FIND YOUR FANTASTIC™

BY

MARCEA WEISS

Calypso Publishing

Digital ISBN 978-0-9912663-0-2

Print ISBN 978-0-9912663-2-6

First Edition

June 2016

I may as well tell you right now, because you'll discover it for yourself as you read ahead, that I think life is a great place. It offers all sorts of opportunities, adventures and new experiences to discover.

Yes, difficult times are sure to pop up from time to time, but they serve a purpose both personally and professionally.

Personally, being backed against a wall is sometimes the only experiences that forces us to choose a direction in contrast to going with the flow or being knocked down. When you are backed into a corner, life requires you to make a decision and take action to clear a new path and direction forward.

Professionally, the same is true. Tough situations require that we make a decision or die. It can make it easier to gain buy in from the team, along the lines of the proverbial "burning platform," and can make the path and need for change, sometimes unpleasant, but clear. Clear can be refreshing.

I often wonder why more people and organizations don't take advantage of all that life has to offer. They seem to be buying time, keeping their head down, just trying to get by. I affectionately refer to these people as "potatoes," and hope to find opportunity to help them off of their coach in the future. Make a continuous effort and celebrate the results , experiences and even downfalls that come from this every day.

How does one best use this book? By reading and doing. Try one thing new in your life from each chapter and be open to where it takes you on your new journey.

I welcome you to the new world to help you to **Find your Fantastic™**

Now, let's get started.

1

One: The Book of Fire
Take action to make the most of today.

1 *T1*

One: The Book of Fire
Take action to make the most of today.

Thought One: Learn from the discovery of fire. Put good ideas to action quickly for the fastest results!

Human ancestors learned to control fire somewhere between 200,000 and 800,000 years ago. This ability allowed drastic changes in our ancestors' quality and way of life. From the ability to stay up past the dark, to increased brain size and scare away predators, it was a big change. Once humans could control fire, people naturally gathered around it to teach and learn skills- to eat and to communicate.

Roughly 20,000 years ago, we developed also a bow and arrow and needle and thread.

10,000 years ago, we learned to make fire by use of flint or fire drills, sticks rubbed together. 400 years ago chemists learned to make matches from urine, toxic as they were.

It took us another hundred years to develop the non-toxic version.

Wow, what a journey! It sure took us a long time to get here didn't it? Can you imagine what a miserable place the world was before we "discovered" or learned to control and then initiate fire on our own? Think about what a difference this discovery made to our ancestors and their quality of life, health and longevity? What took them so long? Was it fear, doubt, a lack of belief in the ability to improve their situation?

Are these same forces active in your life? How can we work beyond them to minimize their effect or eliminate them all together?

If we think of the greatest discoveries, thoughts or goals of our time, let's make sure that we don't take the full 200,000 years to put them in place.

In this book, Find your Fantastic, you will discover new ideas to put in place in your life, to make a difference in your life.

Let's take action today!

1 *T2*

One: The Book of Fire
Take action to make the most of today.

Thought Two: You can do anything but you can't do everything.

I enjoy reading books and talking with other successful people, asking for their advice and learning more about how they got where they are today. In doing these things, we are presented with many more ideas that can be immediately implemented.

This is to be expected. When we are tuned in to the possibilities of life, tuned in to making continuous improvement in ourselves and our organizations, we'll encounter many more ideas, activities and actions then we can reasonably act upon or put in place.

When this happens, we must make a choice. Think simple and to the point. Walk forward with a bias toward action. Choose your best alternative and test it out.

A wise man and founder of the Toyota Production System that was key in setting the ground work to allow Toyota to become the #1 automobile manufacturer in the world- an idea un heard of in the 1980s, think "YO" trucks bopping down the street. Taiichi Ohno, considered one of the forefathers of these improvements trained his teams to test things out, to stop talking and start doing. He encouraged his teams, saying that most people are wrong 50% of the time.

With this in mind, it is a big waste of time to sit for any amount of time and debate the best course of action.

Test them out and discover from these results which is the best path to follow. Just get started moving in the right general direction.

When life and choices get complicated, force them to be simple by thinking like a child.

Consider what an 8 year old would do. How would they boil down the challenge and the need for action? How would they, in their own innocent way, boil down the options into the simplest next step. When you've determined this, try it out.

The only way to predict that nothing will improve with 100% accuracy is to do nothing, to change nothing.

We know that there are a lot of choices in life on what we can do and how to spend our time. We can't do it all, so we must test out opportunities to see what, "clicks," but how do we know where to start?

Start with what you enjoy in life. What do you feel driven or an inner desire to try out and explore. Start there.

If you've never gotten out to explore, then start there. Try out some new things. Find out what you enjoy, what challenges you and allows you to grow and have a try at it.

1 *T3*

One: The Book of Fire
Take action to make the most of today.

Thought Three: See the big picture. It can be so easy for us to be caught in our current situation, our current perspective, but don't let this happen to you. Today is not forever and the things that you yearn for today are the situations that you've dreaded in the past, or, possibly will in the future.

If you have spent time in the seasonal climates, think of the intense heat in the summer and the extreme cold in the winter. Have you ever longed to be able to interchange a few days back and forth between the two seasons?

Unfortunately, we are not given this option very often. Let's learn to enjoy what we have while we have, yet plan for the future and the changes that are sure to come. Let's not live in the moment of always looking for what we don't have. What a waste that is to observe!

Let's live in the moment, grateful for what we've got, taking steps to achieve our desired future.

1 *T4*

One: The Book of Fire
Take action to make the most of today.

Thought Four: So, we all know that Olympic and world class athletes write down their goals. Many business leaders do also. Do you?

Have you done this in your life? If you have, you've probably noticed the incredible results. You can feel your subconscious going to work for you to put into place the situation that you envisioned, that you described. You can see how your mind finds every opportunity to contribute to your vision.

If you have not yet tried this, start small. Write down your expectations for the next 12 months. What will have changed? What will have improved? How will life and family look and feel different? Why will it matter?

Write it down in words or cut out pictures and paste them to a Vision Board to create the future reality in pictures. Think not only about how, concretely, this future will be different for you and your loved ones, but how it will feel and what difference it will make in your lives.

Start today by asking what is important to you? Where would you like to be one or five years from now? Write it down.

Writing it down is important for two reasons. First, it makes sure that you have identified actual specific goals instead of vague or implied goals. Second, it puts your self-conscious to work for you. I am no psychologist, but I have seen first-hand the power of the unseen mind while training, studying and preparing for future achievements in the military as well as in sports and professional life.

When working to gain the attention of national team rowing coaches, I was working on my finish. This is the part of the rowing stroke where your arms come in to your body, cycle around and then lead your body's way back up the slide to take another bite of water. My coach had given me input at the end of the previous week, telling me not to "break my wrist," or keep them flat, at their best supported position. This was not natural for me.

The following week, during practice, she complemented me on my improvement and asked what had changed. I recalled with her my memory of a dream where I'd been sitting on a sidewalk rehearsing a good finish over and over again, without the side effect of a sore backside from all that time on the concrete!

On another occasion in the military, when I was studying to make Pilot in Command (PC) for the first time, my barracks roommate let me know that I had woken her up in her sleep the night prior. I had been reciting all of the emergency procedures and systems limitations that are key to PC status, signing for the keys and taking charge of your own UH-60 Blackhawk and crew. I was happy to hear this. "What an efficient system," I thought. Mastering the topics needed while resting!

When you write down your goals and visualize the future that these accomplished goals create, it puts your mind, body and spirit to work in ways that I don't completely or need to fully understand to make them a reality.

So, you've set some remarkable goals and are now excited to see them come to life. Now, I have a strange request. Don't worry if they don't come to pass in exactly the same manner, time line or results as you had hoped or requested. Make room for the unexpected and value the path that it will create.

Earlier in my life, I would plan and rehearse, then think, and plan some more. This would cause a lot of extra thought and effort with some stress when things would not follow the path that I had hoped or envisioned.

What I found at the other end was the remarkable part. It was not so much that my dreams or hoped had changed, but they came to life in completely unexpected ways, ways that I was not able to envision. In better and more creative ways than I could have expected or even mapped out on my own if I had tried. Make room for the serendipity of life.

1 *T5*

One: The Book of Fire
Take action to make the most of today.

Thought Five: Plan your next step; Not Next year. We've already talked about how smart people are wrong half of the time and that plans don't usually follow the plan, but great results happen anyway in often unexpected ways.

Let's not spend our time mapping out the detailed plan for the next 40 years. Let's think about our 1 to 5 year plan with 80% accuracy and then boil it down to what I need to be doing right now to move in that direction.

That's right, don't focus on everything that needs to be done to set your vision to life, but only think about the next thing that needs to be done and then work to accomplish it. Be open to the new information that presents itself along the way. Don't give up on your end vision, but be open to reaching it in unique ways with an updated timeline.

I remember coming home from school in the 3rd grade and mom asked how it went. My twin sister and I shared our frustration and sense of overwhelming that we had after our teacher had assigned us a 6 line poem to commit to memory that night. We could not imagine it. That was the problem. Here it is, by memory:

> *Oh, there once was a puffin just the shape of a muffin that lived in the island in the bright blue sea.*

> *He ate little fishes that were most delicious and he had them for supper and he had them for tea.*

> *But their poor little puffin, he couldn't play nothing' for he hadn't anybody to play with at all.*

So, he sat on his island and he cried for a while and he felt very lonely and he felt very small.

Then, along came the fishes and they said if you wishes you can have us for playmates instead of for tea.

Now, they all play together in all sorts of weather and the puffin eats pancakes like you and like me.

Mom, said, "nonsense, let's get started," and you can see it worked. Mary and I were the only ones in the class that had the whole poem memorized the next day, and the next 30+ years, and mom taught us a valuable lesson on getting started by taking the first step. Thanks Mom!

80% to me, by the way, means looking at all of the alternatives and all that needs to be done and boiling it down to the top 3-5 items that are the most important. Very rarely do we as individuals or as organizations have enough capacity to do it all.

We must make this decision every day whether we choose to do it pro-actvely or as a victim of our inability to decide. BE open to and accepting of the idea that some things will not get done. Sometimes I will say, "no." Let's get involved with this decision!

Let me tell you about a pet peeve of mine. I call them "busy people." On occasion, people in the professional world have commented or accused me of being "busy." I correct them quickly. That's not me.

That's not you either. No one is busy. Everyone has the same amount of time in every day.

We can choose to make a decision now to spend it, or, hopefully, invest it. Think about it. We have 24 hours today and tomorrow and the next day, etc. That is a heck of a lot of time!

Think about it.

What if you had to lay out a plan right now of how you were going to spend that time? 24 hours today. 24 hours tomorrow. All of next week? How about next month or year? Wow, that is a lot of time you have on your hands! When we really think about it, it's not so much having enough time, but really making the right decision on how to spend it.

Think also about people who operate at higher levels than you do in your organization or in your community.

How do they manage to get it all done? The answer is simple, really. They don't. They plan what they'll do and do what they plan. Everything else will go away or it will wait.

Sometimes, I think it is easier to worry that we will run out of things to do or will stop being occupied. That would be tough! Kind of gives you a new perspective, doesn't it?

The key to not being or becoming a busy person is to make a decision on what is important to you and spend your time there.   How do we do this? Refer back to thought #2 for ideas to get started.

When an individual responds to any of your requests by telling you how busy there are, what they are really saying is that your request is not important enough for me or they do not know what is important to them.

Don't be a busy person. Decide what is important to you and invest your time in these areas. When requests come up that are not a priority, be pleasant, but direct, in letting the organization or individual know that this is not something that you are able to support at the moment. You can let them know that you see the importance and wish them luck, but don't beat around the bush with the excuse of being busy.

My suggestion is to remove it from your vocabulary.

Be open to the expectation that in order to reach that goal, I work to take the next step in that direction (even if the goal seems miles away) and understand that some days will feel more like a step to the side or even back, but the important thing is to get up every day and take that step!

In my first book, <u>Leaving the Military; Your Deployment Guide to Corporate America</u>, I shared a graph or how I view the general curve of input of effort to output of results. We can have the mistaken impression that 1 unit of input should yield 1 unit of output. I have found that to generally not be the case and we should not expect it. Life does not yield linear results.

There is one linear equation that we can bank on. Zero units of input will most certainly yield zero results. Yes, we've mentioned this earlier, but it's important enough to re-visit.

We have to plan for an irregular plot of output, despite our constant level of input. Expect a plateau from time to time, acceleration forward or a couple of steps to the side.

If you are a gardener, you'll understand this concept. You can plant the same garden, in the same soil, with the same effort, even rotating the plant positioning to minimize soil deprivation, but you won't get the same harvest. Some years will be a bumper crop and others will be less. The common denominator is maximum and continued effort.

Plan for this and you won't be disappointed.

1 *T6*

One: The Book of Fire
Take action to make the most of today.

Thought Six: It is important to stretch to reach the next level and to compete. What is your race track?

If you've participated in sports, you understand the importance of stretching beyond your most recent best record, to push yourself. In running, this was known as sprint training or "fartlek" interval training (great word to have ready for Balderdash, by the way, one of my favorite board games!)

With this sort of interval training, you break your training routine (rowing, running, writing a book, etc.) into shorter, multiple intervals than the entire task or event requires. During the interval, you push your mind or body to operate at a higher level that it has in the past. Surely, you can do this for only 30 seconds vs. the overall 7 minute total? (This is what you tell yourself). Then you repeat this training for the needed number of intervals to reach the total vs. running at an even pace for the entire distance.

This training teaches your mind, body and spirit how to operate at a higher level, how to operate at the next level and to get comfortable doing it.

As your output increases, increase the length of your interval. As the interval length reaches the overall event length, you've just successfully trained yourself to operate at the next level!

If you've never done this before, it may sound all too simplistic, but come on, you have to know this is possible. Michael Jordan did not wake up one day doing slam dunks!

This is the same in life. How can we expect to improve our performance professionally without planning for the same training?

This means we must help ourselves to get comfortable getting out of our comfort zone, to get comfortable not being the 'seasoned expert.' We have to be Ok with not getting it right the first time, with failing as we learn to do it right.

Think back to the times in your life when you pushed the limit and surprised yourself by accomplishing the task.

We don't really get to know what our limits are if we never push beyond them, to find the current limit of our capability.

We can't win them all but we won't win any if we don't go out on the field and show up to make an effort.

Start today to train yourself to see every failure as getting you one step closer to success, as a necessary part of the journey to reaching the results that you desire. Along with the old sales adage, "Every 'no' is one step closer to a 'yes.'"

Teach yourself to make note of how many failures you've had over the past day, week, month, year or more. How many have there been? If your answer is zero, get worried.

One of my grade school teachers selected me to attend a science camp one summer in a remote part of the country. It was fun. We did experiments and learned new things such as the term Forensic Microscopy and more.

I had a powerful lesson on taking action when one of the counselors stood in front of the big group and did a rope trick. She let us know that she'd be challenging us to compete to recreate it in order to win a prized bag of M&M candies. She had my attention.

It started with 3 ropes of varying sizes and by the end, the counselor "magically" made them the same size as she counted them and showed them to us in front of the group.

She displayed the rope trick a number of times and then asked the group who was ready to demonstrate it back to her. Fortunately, I had noticed one key item when observing. I could see how two of the ropes could be folded and looped together to make up the same dimension of the third rope, but I did not see the whole answer.

Excited by the observation, I raised my hand and rushed to the front of the room. I stood in front of the counselor and recreated what I had observed- fold two ropes and loop together to make all three ropes the same size.

He answer was, "good, now what?" What happened there has had me thinking for many years. As she asked the question, the answer came to me. It was a matter of counting the ropes in the right order. I used the single rope to count, "1," and then the double rope, after a smooth swap, to count, "2," and then all together to count, "3."

I never would have accomplished this if I had not taken the risk to try and put myself in the right place at the right time to try and to succeed. I also had to be open to the possibility to not be successful.

Try harder. Try new approaches. They don't have to have been tried before.

Get Ok with experiencing ambiguity, testing things out to learn that they don't work and to move on to the next approach that will yield unprecedented results.

1 *T7*

One: The Book of Fire
Take action to make the most of today.

Thought Seven: Why I love potatoes and why you should not be one. Oh my gosh, have you ever had a garden? Did you ever plant potatoes? They are the best! I loved them as a kid and find that our family gets just as exc ted when we plant and harvest them in the garden.

Picture it. The mounds are still present. The plant has gone past its prime and visibly drying up. It's fall and the rest of the garden has also come to a stand-still. Time to dig up the potatoes!

Get a shovel and assemble your team. Hopefully some of them are under the age of 5 because this adds a whole new level of excitement. Give a safety brief because it is about to get exciting and you don't want to have any little fingers competing with the shovel.

Ok, spade up a pile of dirt at least a foot away from the base of the dwindling plant. Turn it over and stand back. Watch the little fingers make their way through the soil. Have a bucket ready to collect the little buggers.

As you are digging, ask them what they'd like to do with the potatoes- Frerch fries, mashed or potato pancakes. Get their imagination going!

If you've never done this before, it is just as exciting as Christmas or Chanukah in July. The potato seeds that were planted "eyes up" in the Spring have now multiplied and you don't get to see them, not even a peak until they are liberated in the Fall.

I hope this story illustrates clearly how much I like potatoes, in this scenario. There is another meaning in my mind for the term potatoes that I dislike just as much as I like this first one.

In travelling, attending conferences, meeting people, I am often amazed at how many people are disengaged in their jobs, in their life in their experiences. Going through the motions, they don't seem energetic or engaged in what they are doing. Sometimes I wonder if they are really even there or if an alien or inflatable double has been put there in their stead.

Whether it is at a sales conference where they linger behind their booth, hoping to not be noticed, or at a company or town meeting where they are lingering behind the table.

It always makes me wonder, what are you doing here? What would you like to be doing? Why don't you get started?

In my mind, I've learned to categorize these people unfortunately as potatoes. It's just the best term that I can visually come up with. Much like looking at a potato, they are just sitting there, not really interacting, not a real part of their life or their surroundings, waiting to be dug up.

Don't be a potato. Break free of this routine before it breaks you. Let's dig you up today to experience sun light and fresh air!

You can break free by getting back in touch with who you are.

What are your dreams? What got you excited as a child? Start by getting involved in an activity once per week that brings back this sense of engagement and desire and then work to grow that time to as much of your day and your life as you can.

I've had jobs where you just get by, not fully challenged, and the jobs where you are fully challenged and engaged and can't help but take some of the work home.

You want to talk with your family and friends about it, to bounce around ideas with others. You want to tinker with finding the best solution or improvement. It's a great feeling! Once you've experienced this type of work, how could you ever go back?

Short term, our work might demand that we do a job that's not our favorite, or keep things moving until other options are available, but if you find yourself in this position long term, find something new. Taking this action will benefit you and the results of your work.

Open the doors to a whole new world where you are an active, engaged part of your professional life and don't look back at the potato mound.

(If you do decide to become a startup potato farmer, regular mounding is recommended for the best crop.)

1 *T8*

One: The Book of Fire
Take action to make the most of today.

Thought Eight: Value your "free exercise" experiences

It's important to be physically active. I am fortunate that growing up on a farm, spending time in national level sports and then in the active military, I learned to make time for exercise or physical exertion.

Time at the gym, walking over lunch, taking the stairs, helping a friend move boxes or even cleaning are great examples. The later examples, I refer to as "free exercise," where you get the exercise that you would at a gym, without paying for it.

As more and more of us move into professional roles, it is even more important that we find ways to build this into our work and personal lives.

Our house is not a museum. We have a lot of activity and a lot going on and a big family of healthy, active people that don't always put things away. This is not my preference. I like to have a clean house, but I like to encourage our family to get involved in things that they love, to take an active role in life more than cleaning and organizing.

I want to ensure as a family that we spend 80% of our time doing the most important things, which to me, is learning, experiencing life and loving each other. I also want to instill good habits and life skills.

I like to clean. It is a simple task that does not require a lot of planning or materials and I am rewarded with almost instant visual gratification of a job well done.

I am fortunate with my background in farming, sports, the military and hands-on work, I value physical activity. If I don't plan something into my day to get my heart rate up, I feel that I missed something.

This time allows me a moment to clear my head and think, to be grateful, to strengthen my vision for the future. It also makes my body feel great, sometimes not until I am done, but it does.

I recommend a combination of physical exercise and meditation or quiet reflection to enable a clear mind, healthy body and energized spirit.

2

Two: The Book of Reflection

It's already inside of you; You have what you need!

2 *T1*

Two: The Book of Reflection
It's already inside of you; You have what you need!

Thought One: Seek to understand and grow the connection with yourself and with others.

It is possible to live life in a way that we think we are isolated and individual, self-made and even self-directed. This is not ideal.

Connecting with others allows you to get the best input ideas and advice on your future goals, as well as to live the most fulfilled life.

I believe that most people want to do good things, work to their full potential and realize the personal and professional benefits that go along with this.

I a so believe that people want something to believe in and, when put in a leadership position or position of influence, it is our job to authentically give this to them.

It is great the amount of personal freedom and individualism that we are afforded in our professional and personal life, but it's important to realize the power of connection in life.

For those that live on their own and don't feel the need for or connection with others, I say, come on potato, wake up. Look around at the miracles happening every day in your body, in nature, in your family. Tell me how you can see it any other way.

When I was pregnant with each of our children, I remember that remarkable feeling of a human being moving around inside of you. You feel the stretching, kicking and hick ups along with them. Unbelievable. It alters your frame of reference on the world. It is such a miracle and forces you to think, if this is possible, what else is possible in the world that at first, I would not consider?

To increase your connection with those around you, look around to see and value the current connection that you have with others in society- friends, family, community and more. See it and value it. Take time to foster and to grow it.

Look for ways to connect with more people. Consider them, understand them and look for ways to support them.

I've noticed as you go along in life, it's cool to set goals and accomplish or exceed them, but it's really cool to have a hand in helping someone else coming along after you, to use the knowledge and experience that you've gained, to help them do the same thing.

This came to light for me when I was leading service teams in cemeteries, working to start the branch, hire the first people, bring in the first account and grow the business.

I had a great Army veteran who worked for me and was also new to the cemetery care industry. We learned the profession together.

Going into the second year working together, I discovered a contest on one of the local TV stations where you could nominate a military veteran in the community to be recognized as an honorable person to be entered in a contest to win a free car, sponsored by Toyota, by the way.

I nominated my colleague and worked with his wife and the community to get him through the first round of online voting to make it to the on air portion where he and four others would be given an envelope randomly, where one would win a new car.

I was not in town when the final contest aired on TV, but got a call from one of our first cemetery clients, who called to give me the results.

He left a suspense building voicemail, letting me know our colleague had not chosen an envelope, just asked to be handed the last one, and as each of the others opened their envelope, it became clear, that he was the winner!

This was eye opening to me because of how exciting it was. I jumped around the hotel room when I heard the news and thought, why was I so excited? I would not be that excited, if I, myself, had won.

I realized this was the true power of helping others along the way. I did not do a lot in this example, just submit a write up and spread the word, but did find it to be a visible example in my life, of how rewarding and fulfilling a connection with others and commitment to their success can really be.

2 *T2*

Two: The Book of Reflection
It's already inside of you; You have what you need!

Thought Two: Take time for nature.

Nature is beautiful, gentle, powerful, simple, limited and unexpected. It's a great analogy for life.

Life is not all linear, much like nature, although when we get where we've been trying to go, we can look back and see an ordered path to get there.

Look for inspiration and answers in what you find in nature.

It's an unlimited path of possible connections, next steps, ordered and unordered that present a model for us to see inspiration and natural ordered decision making that seeks out the simplest path, through unlimited options, to the future.

The value ins setting aside time for nature it to allow us to release ourselves from the present day, to understand that we are not the only controlling force in the world, but also to seek new inspiration and thoughts on what is really possible.

We can find models for the solutions of the problems that we face today in nature, who has already found an efficient solution in the ages of history that has created it.

2 *T3*

Two: The Book of Reflection
It's already inside of you; You have what you need!

Thought Three: Follow your natural curiosity. There is something to it.

Our parents and teacher taught us to buckle down and get our work done. This is important for sure, but we must also plan time to continue to play and explore.

Do you recall experiencing as a child the exiting and empowering world of a new toy or play ground or unexplored environment? What did that feel like? How did you respond? Did you reserve yourself in this environment to what is possible and what is not, time constraints, budgetary, logical constraints, or did you just get started in learning, exploring and growing?

Do you recall that feeling of uninterrupted focus and excitement with a lack of fear, doubt or desire to talk yourself out of making the first step?

How often do you experience this today?

What could you do to re-create this experience today in professional and personal life in order to grow?

2 *T4*

Two: The Book of Reflection
It's already inside of you; You have what you need!

Thought Four: See how you help others; Help yourself.

I grew up on a dairy farm in Wisconsin and had the opportunity to help out with a wide variety of chores, tasks and problem solving daily.

It was an annual rhythm of keeping up with the daily chores of feeding, milking, cleaning, removing waste balanced with the annual rhythm of planting, fertilizing and harvesting crops to allow the daily life to continue.

I recall one afternoon when my dad climbed up the side of our highest silo, up the external cage to complete some maintenance and remove one of the panels that allowed access as the level of feed inside reduced with the year. I watched from a hay wagon below, ready to run for a tool or assist as needed, uneventfully.

When dad came down from the silo, we went in by mom for lunch, where dad shared a brief summary with mom. He had been nervous climbing up to the top height of the silo, leaning back on the cage while he removed the panel and complete the maintenance. He said as he looked over at me watching him that my calm expression and that calmed him as he worked.

I'm not sure why this experience stuck with me, but it did. We are powerful and impactful in ways that we don't always understand. Our presence and demeanor and beliefs can make a big difference.

This experience helped me to understand the importance of positive thinking, faith, willingness to help and what a difference it can make sometimes just being there.

I also learned the importance of development, grooming for the future and setting expectations. On the farm, all the working age workers that weren't mostly moved out of the house, were my sisters and I, a background that helped me to avoid any experience or grooming to think that male and female roles were different.

My dad was also a great help with this as he had goals for each of us- to be sure we'd be able to milk the herd of cows on our own, back up a two wheel wagon (the manure spreader under the barn cleaner) and more.

Dad's dad, grampa, aslo groomed him to be a hard worker. Grampa worked a job in the city, as a movie projectionist and then hunted, fished and trapped to augment the family income.

Grampa bought a farm for dad when he was 14 and would drop him off in the country to farm for the day, provide value to the family and to keep him out of trouble, he said.

Dad let us know that his goal was to be the toughest person that we'd ever work for in order to make life easier in the future. I think this was a valuable goal, and he did reach it for the most parts, but I let him know that, in some cases, he could have tried harder because there are some remarkable bosses out there.

I also had the value of growing up with a handful of remarkable sisters, who from time to time, I'd find myself looking at with admiration, thinking they were some pretty great ladies.

When I'd do that (and I'm sorry up front if this sounds selfish), I'd think to myself, they are similar to me in background, work, personality, accomplishment, etc. This was somewhat of a mathematical proof to myself during times of low self-esteem to bring me back up and to be confident and positive.

Again, I'm not a psychologist, but my lesson learned here is to find ways to see yourself through positive eyes. If you are not your own best friend, encouraging, talking positive talk to yourself, then change. Look in the mirror and find something that you like every day and tell yourself. Provide encouragement and love. (Just a suggestion, do this for your external friends too!)

Again, we don't always know what sort of impact we are having on others as well as ourselves, by being positive, being present, making a difference by connecting with them.

2 *T5*

Two: The Book of Reflection
It's already inside of you; You have what you need!

Thought Five: Be mentally ready and resilient, reflect and meditate. Watch for and listen to the ideas that come to you. Act on the ones that persist. Learn to focus this attention and refine it as you go along in life.

Ok, so I've been kicking around this book for the better part of six years. I've outlined the chapters, looked at book formatting, typed some every few months or years or so and tried to drop it (really).

And, it won't go away, so here I am.

The nagging idea and resilient themes won't go away until I complete them on papers. You can see that they don't have to be perfect in order to be satisfied, but I am doing my best!

I believe that these nagging ideas are there for a reason and although it does sometimes feel like a cowboy is chasing me around the rodeo ring with a lasso, I am thankful that they come to me. It is one of the ways that I know that I am connected to the world in more ways than I completely understand, or will ever completely understand in this world.

Have you ever woken up in the middle of the night to jot down an idea that came to you or called a friend to discuss?

When they come to you, consider the source of the desire to be sure it is good, and then value these ideas and act on them. They are coming to you for a reason.

Just be aware that once you act on them the funnel is open and more will come. Be patient but persistent with yourself as you drive them to completion and have fun while you do it.

2 *T6*

Two: The Book of Reflection (water is the visual symbol, simple, tough, persistent, powerful)
It's already inside of you; You have what you need!

Thought Six: Connect with the importance of your work to update and discover new opportunities.

See through the surface of what life is asking you to do and be open and ready for new challenges that present themselves. It's invigorating!

I've shared openly that when you look at my resume, there are more career stops than I would have designed if given the opportunity map my own course completely.

Some changes were chosen by myself or a family decision based on other opportunities or geography. On one occasion, an employer informed me unexpectedly that my services were no longer needed at the organization.

I've worked in many industries from high tech and media sales, health care to death care and manufacturing. I am grateful for each stop along the way and gained valuable experience and connections on each occasion.

At each stop, it was interesting to see, and I learned to minimize, much of the critique from others. "Aren't you overqualified for that?" "Should an electrical engineer work on this?," "What does a helicopter pilot have to do with _____?" "Where is that job likely to lead?"

I had a reason for each stop, valued the experience and felt a connection with enough of the people on the team to want to dig in and make a difference and an improvement in the multiple customers, both internal and external that were involved along the way.

The experience taught me that life is about more than a job title. It is important to me to continue to progress and grow and see advancement in my career overall, but it can come in different shapes, sizes, locations and job titles and there is value in that.

I've also learned to value you others' input in life decisions, but only to a certain level and then make my own decisions.

I'm not living to fulfill their goals or to live their dreams and their thoughts and advice is based on looking at my life through their lenses, which is not an accurate view.

Find the importance and connection with meaning for the work that you are doing today.

Life is too short.

The people and customers that you are interacting with are relying on you to be present and engaged, to work toward your full potential. You are mostly hurting yourself if you are going through the motions, trying to ignore the fact that you are not fulfilled or living with a purpose.

If you are not engaged and giving 100% of what you are capable of giving today, you are hurting yourself and those around you.

When you get to the place where you can work to your full potential and show your authentic self, you will understand the gap, and wonder why you waited so long to go there.

3

Three: The Book of Adversity
Destroy your limits, in doing so discover yourself!

3 *T1*

Three: The Book of Adversity

Destroy your limits, in doing so discover yourself!

Thought One: See the value in adversity. It pushes you up against a wall and forces you to decide what is important to you. What direction will you emerge? You can no longer wander in any direction at this point.

End results are often better than what you planned or expected. Value this

I can't help but sharing a dating example here, although will never claim to be your expert here.

When I was on active duty in the military, I moved every 1 to 3 years for 10 years, resulting in roughly 7 different addresses during that time. I was also young and single and dating. These types of moves could be looked at as detrimental to a young 20 something, but in contrast, as I observe others' dating lives after leaving the military, I saw the value.

A relationship would start and it either advanced or discontinued based on a pending move.

I observe other young people who are in a relationship for 5 or more years, wondering what the next step is and if it will arrive.

The adversity in the constant military moves added a healthy consideration of whether or not the relationship would continue. If it was not moving forward, it was going to stop. Why go through all that work to maintain a relationship that was not going anywhere?

Looking back, this was healthy and I'm thankful for it. I'm not sure that I would have come up with these ground rules on my own, but with the added adversity, they were natural.

When working through my own professional career transition from the military to the civilian world, it was awkward at first. It felt as if I was the only one who'd be leaving active duty that year, although about 200,000 active and another 200,000 reserve forces do this annually.

At first, this added stress and made the transition more difficult. In the end, it was a blessing, as it forced me to really think about what kind of career I desired. What type of opportunity and company was I looking for?

People wanted to know how flying a helicopter would be useful in their civilian, non- rotary wing organization. It was my job to set a professional goal and re-frame the conversation to share my specific experiences that proved that I was a fit.

After completing it, and looking from the other sides back, I wrote a book on the topic title, <u>Leaving the Military; Your Deployment Guide to Corporate America</u>. This book allows me to assist many other military veterans looking to make the same transition, a fulfilling and rewarding effort.

Without the initial discomfort and adversity, this would not have been possible.

3 *T2*

Three: The Book of Adversity
Destroy your limits, in doing so discover yourself!

Thought Two: As goals are set higher and challenges get tougher, doubt is more natural the closer you get to a breakthrough. Expect this and dig in when it happens, keep moving forward.

My sister Mary shared a card that dad sent to her when she was fighting her way through Air Force Basic Training. The goal in military basic training is to break you down to build you back up as a new person, with new discipline, a better understanding of the military culture and norms, and commitment toward the teams' goal. The card said, "It's always darkest before dawn," and she found it meaningful keeping a hold of it all of these years.

It's the last 10% that makes a difference- in achieving personal, professional and sports goals and in reaching new limits.

I've entertained myself with the experience of flying as a professional military rotary wing pilot once in a combat zone, and as a civilian fixed wing Cessna pilot.

When flying as a civilian in a small Cessna airplane, you can hear it in the air traffic controller's voice that they don't have high expectations in what you are planning to do with the aircraft. This is especially true when you announce that you are a "student pilot." You can almost hear in their voices, "Come on Cessna, get it going…"

When you are part of a UH-60 Blackhawk crew, the amount of detail put into planning the flight, standardizing the checklist, practice in talking with controllers has all of the same high- level moving parts as that of a small plane pilot: preflight, gas, fuel sample, radio calls, log book, etc.   But the result and environment is very different.

The environment is different because it has been defined differently with different expectations.

You have to start by asking yourself what level of achievement you are looking to deliver. Are you the Cessna put-putting down the runway or a UH-60 Blackhawk delivering combat power?

The steps can look the same, but the intent and results will vary greatly by that last 10% of detail and planning that will go into your work.

3 *T3*

Three: The Book of Adversity
Destroy your limits, in doing so discover yourself!

Thought Three: Don't waste your time looking at and evaluating what others are doing and why. Wish them the best. Try to help them, but don't try to get in their head or to pull them into yours.

Most don't follow this path. They can't help but watch and judge, spending most of their time observing others' choices, critiquing and judging them, adding commentary as they go.

What a waste of time. I encourage them to get in the ring and take a few rounds on their own. It's a whole different world to observe from the sidelines than it is to get in the ring, lead the effort and live or die on you and your team's own results and learnings.

What is truly fixed and non-negotiable in your life? What is on your list of "never's?" Why are those limits there? Is it a limit that you have placed or someone else? Is it based on fear, on what is not acceptable, on someone else's expectations or judgements?

What are you really trying to accomplish in your life? What will it take to get there? Which of these items conflict with your list of "never's?"

As life goes along, we realize how important it is to not make it a priority to fit in, but it is more important to set goals and take the next step to arrive at that destination.

When I'd completed my first tour of duty with the 25th Infantry Division in Hawaii, I went on to military professional training, classes included leadership, staff functions, planning, communicating, etc. One course that I greatly desired was not on the list. It was the Maintenance Test Pilot course and I was completely hooked on it as I'd met warrant officers performing in this role in my unit in Hawaii.

I felt that it was the ultimate role in that it involved test flying the aircraft after it came out of significant maintenance or repair procedures. One of the things that has kept me connected to and motivated about Army Aviation is the technology included on the air frame.

How do we keep a power train system that rotates at 20,000 RPMs in some place and 258 RPMs in other completely balanced and stable at a 10 foot hover?

From the chip detectors that remove ferrous material from the transmission fluid, to the ballistic protection of the fuel line, thermocouple engine temperature sensor and non-destructive testing that keeps us informed of pending material failures, I think it's exciting.

When I learned that there is a role where you bring together maintenance teams that have performed this maintenance and systematically check to be sure all systems are in order and air worthy from ground checks to manipulating the power control levers in flight to check maximum performance, I thought that was for me- a great connection with my engineering degree as well.

Unfortunately, not everyone agreed. My rank was wrong as I was commissioned and not a warrant. The timing was wrong as I had fewer Pilot in Command hours than what was required and the school house had changed the policy, not allowing commissioned officers to attend in flight status.

Somehow, while on site at Ft. Rucker, I was able to find a seat to observe the class from the back seat. There were a few times where this seemed worse than not taking the course at all, since it was almost a teaser. I could observe the pilots in the front going over the maneuvers, and study with them, but could not put my hands on the controls to actually do them. People asked me if this was frustrating.

I did what I am recommending that you do. I put my head down and kept taking steps forward in the direction that I felt was best to reach the goal. It did not have to make sense to others.

When I arrived at my next unit, part of the 1st Infantry Division in Germany, I'd ask for advice from more seasoned pilots and maintenance pilots on how I might complete this course requirement and become a maintenance test pilot. They would say, boy, I don't know. You could go back to the course, keep asking for it, or you could challenge the course, without much confidence in either one.

Challenging the course meant that you would contact the standardization pilots at the main US Army school house and let them know that you feel that you can test out of the requirements without attending the school- pretty gutsy.

I kept asking the questions over the next two years in Germany and came up with the best alternative to allow me to move forward, which really seemed in my eyes to be a long shot. I reminded myself that they only way to make no progress was by doing nothing and I moved forward on this alternative.

My team in Germany helped me to prepare with local training and then coordinate training with our in-country standardization pilot and finally to coordinate for a check ride with the overall US Army standardization pilots when they were next in Germany.

I was the first one to challenge the US Army UH-60 Blackhawk Maintenance Test Pilot course, which was confirmed by the letter that the head instructor wrote to me when complete. It said they had chosen to give me a graduation date with the class that had me observing in the back of the aircraft as no one had ever challenged this course before and they weren't sure how to handle it.

Again, thank you adversity for helping to define a new path!

So many steps that I took and take in life did not make sense to others. From joining the military to leaving the military; from staying home with children to going back to work; from working in cemeteries or any number of industries and locations to working for myself.

The more you flex the muscle to take calculated risks and make decisions that make the most sense for you and your family, vs. the critic, the more you have the courage to do this at a greater rate in the future.

3 *T4*

Three: The Book of Adversity
Destroy your limits, in doing so discover yourself!

Thought Four: Don't suffer multiple opportunities and the consequences that go along, Value them

One of the toughest decisions that I had to make early on in life was to decide to leave the US Army World Class Athlete Program (WCAP), Rowing and get started in flight school.

In a way, it was exciting, because I was really motivated to get going on learning to fly and learning more about my future life in the military.

In another way, I was closing the door on training for the Olympics and any chance to be in Atlanta in 1996.

I choose to leave as I felt that the odds where high that I would not make the team after placing a distant 2nd in the women's single scull event at the Pan Am trials in Knoxville, TN. I also was concerned that if I waited too long, the Army would give away my slot at flight school and I would not get to fly.

I should mention that I worked very hard to get to the World Class Athlete program as it was an undefined path for rowing and I did not know anyone who had done this before.   Sometimes the amount of work invested can be a hindrance in changing course, but we have to avoid this.

People, family members, told me that this was a once in a lifetime opportunity that I should not give up on easily. This was true, so was flight school.

I've learned that big decisions are a lot like little decisions. You have information going in, a prioritized list of what you'd like to get out of the other end and also a gut feeling that should be incorporated.

Life requires us to be comfortable in the world of ambiguity. We don't get a guarantee on the outcome, just a best estimate and a gut feeling that can't always be measured. I put about 80% emphases on the roughly measured inputs and outputs and 20% emphasis on the gut feeling make a decision and move on.

3 *T5*

Three: The Book of Adversity
Destroy your limits, in doing so discover yourself!

Thought Five: At some point in all of our professional and personal lives, we will likely experience organizations or people who just don't want us around anymore. When this happens, work to clarify, don't jump to conclusions, but also don't hesitate to move on when that's the best choice.

Take it as a sign that it may be time to move on and avoid taking it personally. Life has a way of continuously sending us messages and inspiration to keep growing, developing and challenging ourselves.

We are not on earth to be friends with everyone or have everyone's approval. We are here to be connected and try to help others. Not everyone wants or is ready to be helped. That is OK.

It is important evaluate your own intentions while making the decision of what to do, being sure they are positive. If your intent is of mal intent, such as getting even or proving people wrong, then stop. Leaving won't accomplish this. But, if you feel you can be better challenged elsewhere or develop and grow in other areas, then consider the change.

Be ok with the people who don't want to be your buddy and don't want your help. There is no need to worry unless you run out of places to work or people to help and that's not likely to happen.

4

Four: The Book of Acceptance

Consider the Serenity Prayer... God, grant me the serenity to accept the things I cannot change, Courage to change the things I can, And wisdom to know the difference.

Learning to accept what is not ideal but I can't change.

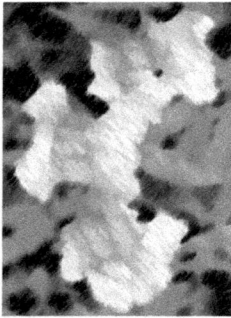

4 *T1*

Four: The Book of Acceptance
Teach me to change what I can and accept what I cannot.

Thought One: Bring others along as you advance and grow. Work with those who are working through similar challenges. Help them to be successful and in doing so, you help yourself.

One thing about setting goals and planning for the future is that once you've written them down, visualize them and start to take the steps to move in that direction, it can be hard to stay patient as growth and progress can take time.

Like harvesting the garden, we are not in complete control of when the results are delivered and in what magnitude.

What can we do in the meantime? Well, the first step is to just take a step back and ensure you have done the prior steps effectively. Be sure you've written down your goals and are being true to yourself in taking forward, sideways and sometimes backward steps to get there.

This thought has nothing to do with giving up and everything to do with being patient and enjoying life as you take appropriate action to achieve your goals.

Then, look for others who are looking to head in the same direction and help them to be successful in doing this also. This can be accomplished by mentoring, getting involved with community groups, establishing your own meet up groups, or getting involved in affinity groups with your employer.

Find others moving in a similar direction and help them to be successful. In return, they will help you to do the same.

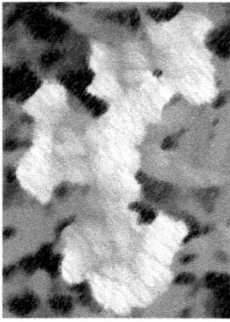

4 *T2*

Four: The Book of Acceptance
Teach me to change what I can and accept what I cannot.

Thought Two: See and accept the good and bad in you and the good and bad in others. Work to continuously improve, but don't expect perfection as it does not exist.

When our son was about 4 years old, he went into my wallet and took $20. When I asked him what happened, he denied it. When I went back again, he denied it again. Finally, he admitted to it as he cried. I let him know what his punishment would be and he ran to his room, hid behind his bed and cried.

I figured this was normal until he was still crying about 15 minutes later, so I went to his room to talk to him. I asked him what was wrong. I let him know that he goofed up, he's being punished and he should focus on what he'd do differently next time. He kept crying.

Finally, I got him to speak and he said that he was not sure he could ever do what mom and dad does. He was not sure that he could ever, "get the naughty's out." I could not believe what he had said.

He had painted a picture in his mind, where at a point in everyone's life, you don't have to choose from doing right or wrong. It just automatically happens because you've learned to be good.

I shared with him that this is not the case, that mom and dad and every adult has to make decisions daily about what is right and what is wrong. The line is usually, but not always, completely clear.

This example and life experience reminded me that it is reality. Daily, we are all looking to make the best decision between what is right and what is wrong, so we should allow some room for people to be people.

We will not always get it right. We'll do it best, but have to make room for in perfections and for mistakes. That's how we all continue to grow, learn and develop.

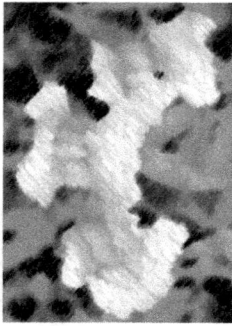

4 *T3*

Four: The Book of Acceptance
Teach me to change what I can and accept what I cannot.

Thought Three: Find out where others are going, goals they have set, efforts they are making to try to improve. Help them along the way.

Remember it is not your path, it is theirs and don't try to force them down yours or into your own head.

Just as we talked in past examples about how we each individually should not allow others to look at our life and our path through their lenses, we should not do that to others.

Give them advice and help out, but remember that they are living their own lives and give them room to do it.

Watch how the outcomes present themselves in different ways than we would expect also.

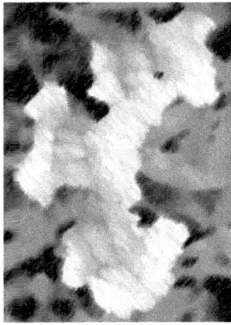

4 *T4*

Four: The Book of Acceptance
Teach me to change what I can and accept what I cannot.

Thought Four: Value you! Talk to yourself and listen to what you are saying.

I've heard it said that when people first listen to the voice that is speaking to themselves in their head, they are surprised by how critical it can be. Perhaps they have recorded the thoughts of a critical parent, unsupportive "friend," negative neighbor or religious leader.

After observing their own internal dialogue, these same people, if given the choice, would not be their own friend.

Think about how you talk to yourself. Be nice. There is only one for sure constant as you go through life, yourself.

Value it.

Appreciate it.

Work to improve it.

Forgive it.

Support it.

Smile at it.

Love it.

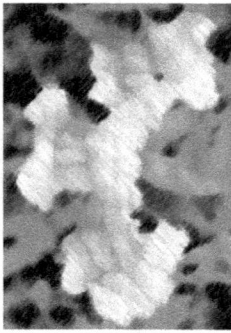

4 *T5*

Four: The Book of Acceptance
Teach me to change what I can and accept what I cannot.

Thought Five: Continue to adjust the lens through which you see life.

Observe your thoughts daily about what you are thinking of others. Are you more positive or negative? Are you looking for good things being done right or bad things and mistakes?

Which are you focusing on, because, in fact, each of us does some good and some not so good things every day.

You will observe and make note of that which you are seeking out.

It's a scary thought and a commoner's opinion, as I'm not a psychologist, but you can create the world that you want to see every day and it effects how you see people and what actions that you take.

If you are surrounded by people who are constantly making mistakes and who don't care about what they are doing, aren't you likely to treat them differently than people who do care and working to make improvements?

I'm not asking any of us to look the other way when performance issues arrive or if we have an outcropping of potatoes that are not engaged in what they are doing.

I am asking us to give people the benefit of the doubt, to ask the potatoes to re-engage, while explaining the performance gap, truly believing in them and their ability to turn it around.

When you run into someone who you work for, that works for you or works with you and they are not performing up to standards personally and professionally, also find ways to wish them well and help them, if at all possible get to where they are going.

Help them get to the place where they can be successful, while shining positive and helpful light in all ways possible.

Leave the table wishing positive thoughts and blessings for them in the future. (Thank you Gino!)

5

Five: The Book of Love and Desire
Love is the most powerful force in the world.

5 *T1*

Five: The Book of Love and Desire
Love is the most powerful force in the world.

Thought One: Ask for advice from others. Listen to it, Take it, consider it, act on it or don't. Give it fair attention and fair consideration.

One of the most powerful questions in the world is to ask, "Can I get your advice?" Particularly if you ask it of people who have gone through similar situations and experiences as you have.

It is powerful because it is a question that benefits the sender and the receiver. The sender benefits from advice that is likely to shorten their path to the level, to reaching their goal.

The receiver benefits because people like to talk about themselves and re-count successes. It inspires confidence and fuels future performance.

5 *T2*

Five: The Book of Love and Desire
Love is the most powerful force in the world.

Thought Two: Keep the childlike perspective.   Remember what it's like to be a child, where you know what you like and can only think about it.

I must have been about 4 years old when I realized how much I like to play. I really liked it and my sisters seemed to have fun also when we were playing together. I'd like to do more, I decided.

The question that I asked myself, was, "how could I do more?" My answer came quickly. I decided to get up in the middle of the night, wake up my sisters and head down stairs.

"Perfect!" I thought. With no interruption, and taking advantage of unused time, it was a real win- win scenario.

My biggest recollection of this life experience was the look on my mom's face as she came downstairs and asked, "What's going on down here?" I was not sure how mom could not recognize or value playing.

Now, being a mom myself, I understand the months and years of sleep deprivation from taking care of the family as well as a herd of cattle that was behind this.

 When you love to do something, your mind and body and spirit will work together to help find a way to make it possible, to make it a reality. That's why it is important to consider what you really enjoy and value in life and increase your time doing this.

Please do insert an intermediate step to ask why you enjoy this activity. What are you motives? Be sure that you get a wholesome and positive response.

If your motives are not positive, something along the lines of getting past someone else, revenge, proving someone wrong, or other, you will not experience long term joy out of this activity.

Think about what you really desire out of life and what you enjoy in it. Think about why. For the areas that give you energy and positive motivation, go after them.

There is a reason these dreams and desires are planted in your heart and a reason why you draw energy from them.

Consider diets that try to deprive you of everything, Not successful.

One of my dad's favorite, only partially untrue, jokes is this:

> My doctor put me on a new and effective diet. He told me that if I put something in my mouth that tastes good, spit it out!

One of his other favorite jokes that is unrelated, but funny and fits him well:

> I visited the dentist the other day with a toothache. When I sat down in the chair to start treatment, I looked at the dentist and said, "We aren't going to hurt each other, are we?"

And finally, my dad's joke that I could not stop telling in grade school, to the point of receiving a detention from Mr. Strong:

> What happened to the bug on the toilet seat? He got pi**ed off!

OK, sorry, I had to go with the moment there, but you can see that I don't believe in 100% compliance. We are here to experience and enjoy life. There is a reason for this.

Allow a divergence from the most direct path from time to time to see and enjoy life.

Parenting taught me so much about people. It's such an amazing experience to have this perfect beautiful bundle of joy show up one day as a miracle in so many ways.

They start to grow and develop. Again, big miracle.

Then, one day, your little miracle, hauls off and hits the other little miracle that's a few years older or younger, and you think, "what happened?"

We realize that the world is not a perfect place. We must give people room to be themselves and to goof up and grow and love them through it all.

Then you watch as others look at your little miracles and see them goofing up, hitting each other, being less than perfect, being themselves and you see the look of disappointment or disgust in their eyes.

It helped me to realize that again everyone trying to do their best every day. We are not ever perfect, but it's better to be our true authentic self than to fake it to be something we are not, something that others are hoping to see.

When I am driving and I see someone acting like a nut or inappropriately, I try to picture them as some other family's little miracle that is having less than a perfect moment and work to treat them the way that I hope the world will treat our little miracles when they goof up.

5 *T3*

Five: The Book of Love and Desire
Love is the most powerful force in the world.

Thought Three: Play! Take time to find good fun! Find humor, laugh, especially with those you love.

The next time you have a good laugh, pay attention to the healing, forgiving, healthy force that is has over everything in your life.

Sometimes, I am certain that I or the world in general plays jokes on myself unconsciously to make me laugh- and it works!

Be able to laugh at your own errors as it helps to bring about the positive s de of our mistakes.

I was stationed in Germany when 9-11 occurred, levelling the World Trade Center and killing so many people in NYC.

Cur lives in the Active Duty Army changed dramatically after that day. After initially being locked down in the aviation facility for most of the night as the situation was monitored, we were allowed to return to our families.

Daily life became a regular rhythm of full military gear, or "battle rattle" and long waits in security lines trying to get on and off post to do our jobs.

Cn one of these occasions, I was driving up to the gate with an old Ford Taurus station wagon that I had brought with me to Germany to see how she would fare on the Autobahn, when I was rolling down the window to d splay my credentials.

The problem was that the window rolled in the opposite direction as our ozher automobile, so as I rode closer to the security guard, I began rolling the window up on top of the other hand and ID badge that I was working to display. I've been laughing at this for years, thinking what it must have looked like to the guard as he observed the lady rolling the window up manually on her own hand.

I can't tell you why exactly it was so funny, but likely my subconscious way of adding humor and positive emotions to a difficult time in our history and for our country.

5 *T4*

Five: The Book of Love and Desire
Love is the most powerful force in the world.

Thought Four: Visualize the future with open imagination. Don't be so realistic in your thoughts that you can't picture it.

One of the first sports that I competed in during high school, after we had left dairy farming and time would allow was track and field.

I ran some short track events and tried my hand a field events- both shot put and discus. I found discus throwing to be really challenging and enjoyable. You could feel when you got it right as it left your hand as it would generate lift and take off down the field.

At one practice session, we arrived to find that they had re-painted the distance lines on the throwing field. Thinking nothing of it, we continued our practice as usual to prepare for the upcoming meet in the next few days.

During the track and field meet, I was surprised by my results, where I ended up medaling in the discus event, the first lady to do this in many years. Our coach asked what changed.

The only thing that had changed, we realized afterword, was that the lines had been painted at different intervals, and farther out on the field. I thought nothing of it as we practiced, expecting myself to reach the line that I always did.

The line happened to be moved at a distance great enough to medal in the event. The experience left me impressed with the power of goal setting and watching for opportunities that I'm not selling my potential short.

6

Six: The Book of Joy and Peace
Joy and peace come from the inside out, not dependent on people or things.

6 *T1*

Six: The Book of Joy and Peace
Joy and peace come from the inside out, not dependent on people or things.

Thought One: I was fortunate to have an experience, or thought, while dating that changed my perspective on the world and on healthy relationships. The thought reminded me that you don't enter a relationship to be happy; you have to be happy before you are in a relationship, in order to be happy in the relationship.

This helped me to realize that joy and peace come from the inside of someone and radiate outward. It can be amplified by external sources, but not created.

It helps me today in considering healthy personal and professional relationships and healthy qualities such as joy and peace. They are generated inside by what you chose to think and do; amplified by the people and places with which you choose to spend your time.

Carrying these thoughts into relationships helps me to make room for thoughts mentioned before, to allow people room to be human.

My sister's first husband is Native American and shared some background in bead work with me when his brothers were in town one day. He showed me how a Native American artist actually plans a flaw into their beadwork and art, representing not only a personal touch, but that humans are not meant to be perfect. It is our flaws that make us unique.

It is great if we can learn to value our own and each other's flaws and strengths in life. The strong relationships strengthen your experience and help you understand how to be happy from the inside out.

If you are uncertain about this thought, picture for a moment, what it would be like to be married to or in a relationship with yourself.

Now, wouldn't you really drive yourself crazy if there were two of you around doing those things that you do?

6 *T2*

Six: The Book of Joy and Peace
Joy and peace come from the inside out, not dependent on people or things.

Thought Two: Don't miss the party. Don't be so caught up in the 'to do' list that you miss the glorious celebration going on around you.

Mom says that when my twin sister and I were born, she had biblical names picked out for us- Mary and Martha.

I thanked her for not naming me Martha, as I could remember very clearly the cow that we had named Martha and where she stood in the barn. She, instead, chose to name me after my God mother and Aunt Marcea.

I do understand the story of Mary and Martha in the bible from a high level, and it seems the name might not have been that far off the mark, as far as I can tell.

When Jesus visited the house, Mary was concerned with entertaining and the experience, where Martha was consumed with the "to-do" list. This is where my focus is likely to fall in life, if I don't monitor myself.

If we spend all of our time, getting things done and "off the list," we miss a lot of the experience and people that life has to offer.

I'm not saying that I'll get rid of my check list, by the way, I'm just saying that I understand that it's important to take time to enjoy the view.

I mentioned the big Army aviation check ride that I took in Germany in order to be signed off as a Maintenance Test Pilot, a dream of mine. As the first standardization pilot showed up in Germany and we began our first check ride, I was more than nervous.

I had the aircraft ready to go and we started the pre-flight inspection together. As we worked our way around the aircraft and climbed to the top to view the hydraulics platform, he asked me to explain what I looked at first when getting on top.

My head started to rush with all of the systems and what to explain first and how to be accurate buy concise. He interrupted my thoughts by explaining that he'd help me out with that question. He said look around to see how beautiful the area and view is.

Then, we jumped into the hydraulic systems.

6 *T3*

S x: The Book of Joy and Peace
Joy and peace come from the inside out, not dependent on people or things.

Thought Three: If you have something that you can't live without, give it away. You are missing the big picture. Prove to yourself that you can live without it.

I ike to pick a day or two every few months and back the truck into the garage and challenge myself and our family to find extra items that have accumulated in the house and donate them.

I find it physically, mentally and spiritually uplifting to make my way back from the donation store with an empty truck knowing that I did a good thing in clearing clutter from our daily lives and also donating items to people who may need them more than we do.

When you have something that you strongly desire, consider experiencing it   Don't hide from it or completely deny yourself.

Like the child that lives with strict rules and finally gets free at college to live it up and flunks out, allow yourself room to experience life.

I don't believe that life has to revolve around 100% compliance or 100% avoidance.

It is a better life to live with balance.

6 *T4*

Six: The Book of Joy and Peace
Joy and peace come from the inside out, not dependent on people or things.

Thought Four: Think about and visualize what is great joy for you. What does it look like? What does it feel like? What do you need to bring it about?

What is joy that connects with your spirit and what are you doing to create this?

Many believe that reflecting with gratitude is a great way to bring it about. Try this. What are you thankful for every day.

It is not likely to be related to gaining material items. If you are considering this, you may want to re-visit your motives and values.

Foster deep joy, not just head, not just heart, but deeper in your spirit. Find it and keep it. Bring it back daily in meditation.

Author's note:

I welcome you to share your ongoing experiences, steps forward, to the side and to the back in your ongoing efforts and our shared vision to assist you to *Find your Fantastic* online at: www.findyourfantastic.com